ADORABLE ANIMAL BABIES

BABY ANIMALS ON THE FARM

SARAH RIDLEY

I0808671

PowerKiDS press

Published in 2026
by The Rosen Publishing Group, Inc.
2544 Clinton Street, Buffalo, NY 14224

First published in Great Britain in 2021
by Wayland

Copyright © Hodder and Stoughton, 2021

Editor: Nicola Edwards
Designer: Lisa Peacock

Cataloging-in-Publication Data

Names: Ridley, Sarah.
Title: Baby animals in the farm / Sarah Ridley.
Description: Buffalo, NY : PowerKids Press, 2026. | Series: Adorable animal babies | Includes glossary and index.
Identifiers: ISBN 9781499453645 (pbk.) | ISBN 9781499453652 (library bound) | ISBN 9781499453669 (ebook)
Subjects: LCSH: Domestic animals--Infancy--Juvenile literature.
Classification: LCC SF75.5 R535 2026 | DDC 636.'07--dc23

All rights reserved.

Every attempt has been made to clear copyright. Should there be any inadvertent omission please apply to the publisher for rectification.

No part of this book may be reproduced in any form without permission in writing from the publisher, except by a reviewer.

Manufactured in the United States of America
CPSIA Compliance Information: Batch #CSPK26. For further information contact Rosen Publishing at 1-800-237-9932.

Find us on

Picture acknowledgements:

Dreamstime: Dorothy Merrimon Crawford 10c, 10b; Kenishirotle 12b. iStock: Anolis01 25t; Balwan 15t; James Bowyer 6b; Drbouz 14t; Fabioski 26b; GlobalP 28tl; Levers2007 9b; Merrimon 29bl; Rotofrank 24t; Patrik Stedrak 8t; Taviphoto 28br; Wicki58 4b. Nature PL: Steve Gettle 23t; Ernie Janes 13; Klein & Hubert 14b, 21t, 27t; Heidi & Hans-Juergen Koch 19t; Roger Powell 25b; Lynn M Stone 20t; Nick Upton 11b. Shutterstock: Nate Allred front cover,1, 29tr; Anneka 11t; Anouska13 6t; Karlie Butler 19b; Christopher Chambers 22b; Coulanges 5c, 29cr; Evan Davies8 4t, 8b; Daniel R Moura 12t; Ian Dumuk 2, 21b; Giedriius 27b; grandbrothers 15b; Margo Harrison 9t; Anton Havelaar 16, 17tl, 18t; Eric Isselee 5b; Jo Jones 7; LittlePerfectStock 29br; Paul Looyen 28tr; Valentina Proskurina 20b, 29cl; Sergej Razvodovskij 29tl; Slowmotiongli 22t,28bl; Andrea J Smith 17r; Stockphoto mania 21c; Studio Dream 3; Andrew Vellar21 18b; Vasily Vishnevskiy 26t; Denis van der Water 24b; Wild Media 5t; kostyantyn_zhuk 23b.

CONTENTS

Words in **bold** are in the glossary on pages 30-31.

FARM BABIES

Baa ... this sheep has **twin** baby **lambs**. Lots of animals are born on farms. Farmers feed them and provide shelter but most of the care is given by the mothers of the baby animals.

Some farmers only keep pigs or cows while others own a mix of animals and their young.

Wild baby animals live on farms, too. These **fox cubs** were born in a **den**.

A mother deer keeps her **fawn** hidden in long grass.

Goslings grow into geese on farm ponds.

LAMBS

A mother sheep is called a ewe. Her lamb grew inside her for five months before it was born. Now she licks her baby clean and learns its smell.

Lambs drink milk from their mother's **udder**.

At first, lambs stay close to their mother. Many ewes have twins or **triplets**.

Soon lambs start to spend time with other lambs.

As they grow up, they nibble grass, rest, and play!

They always return to their mother for more milk. They find her by calling to her ... *baaaa.* She calls back with a low *baaaa.*

As their lambs grow stronger, the ewes show them where to find good grass and shelter from rain or snow.

KIDS

Baby goats are called **kids**. Their mother hides them in the grass for the first week of their lives. She returns to let them drink milk from her udder.

A mother goat is called a doe. This doe is smelling her kid to make sure it is hers. She makes a low *maah* sound and her kid answers with a high *maah*.

Kids like to **headbutt**, run, and leap. This helps them grow stronger and learn how to behave with other goats in the **herd**.

As the weeks pass, kids drink less milk and nibble more grass and leaves. They will always recognize their mother if they stay on the same farm.

PIGLETS

A mother pig, or sow, makes a nest of straw before she gives birth. Her **pregnancy** lasts three months, three weeks, and three days! Her **piglets** are covered in soft hairs.

Each piglet has its own **teat**. About once an hour, the sow grunts to let her piglets know she is about to lie down to let them drink her milk.

A sow touches noses with her piglets. She knows their smell and they recognize her grunts.

These piglets live outdoors. At first piglets just feed and sleep. After a few days, their mother starts to move around more ... and the piglets follow.

A sow feeds her piglets milk for up to 12 weeks. She can sleep while they feed.

Piglets explore together and learn how to be part of a herd.

They copy their mother to learn how to root around for tasty things to eat.

CALVES

In a barn, a cow is licking her newborn **calf**. The calf developed inside its mother for nine months. That is the same amount of time as it took for you to be ready to be born.

The calf *moos* and **nuzzles** a teat to get the milk flowing.

The cow quietly *moos* at her calf. It learns the sound of its mother.

Cows lick their calves to **groom** them and show **affection**.

On some farms, a calf stays with its mother for several months. It continues to drink milk but also **grazes** grass.

When it is tired, a calf rests but its mother is never far away. She will protect it from danger.

Sometimes cows leave their calves with another cow babysitter while the cows go off to graze.

Calves make friends with other calves and play games with them. This helps them find out how they fit into the herd.

CHICKS

This hen lives in a farmyard. She has found a good place to lay her eggs. She sits on them until it's time for her **chicks** to **hatch** 21 days later.

A hen has to **mate** with a rooster for her eggs to hatch into chicks. Most hens do not live with roosters so their eggs can never become chicks.

As she walks around, a hen makes soft *cluck-cluck-cluck* noises to keep her chicks close. She shows them what is good to eat.

As it grows, a chick's soft **down** changes into adult feathers.

Most chicks live in barns rather than with mother hens.

BARN BABIES

High in the roof of this barn, barn owls bring voles, mice, and shrews to their **owlets**.

By the time they are about two months old, the owlets will have grown adult feathers and learnt how to fly.

A pair of swallows built this nest from mud and grass. They bring insects to their chicks for about 20 days until they are ready to leave the nest.

Down in the hay, some tiny **kittens** are asleep in a heap. Their mother will teach them how to hunt and groom themselves.

DUCKLINGS

Some farms have ponds. In spring, this female duck made a nest nearby. She laid eggs and kept them warm for about 28 days until her **ducklings** started to hatch.

After a few hours of life, the duck leads her ducklings to water. Her ducklings follow her wherever she goes and know which duck is their mother.

Quack! The mother warns her ducklings they are in danger. They swim closer to her.

At night she keeps them warm. By day she shows them what to eat. Ducklings stay with their mother until they are about two months old.

HEDGEROW BABIES

As well as fields and meadows, farms have **hedgerows, banks,** and woodland. Here wild animals have babies.

Birds build nests in trees and hedges to keep their eggs and chicks safe. For two weeks, this bird and its mate will feed their chicks with insects.

Caterpillars hatch from eggs laid by butterflies. They never meet their parents.

Harvest mice build nests for their young among the stems of plants.

Baby rabbits are blind and naked at birth. After two weeks they start to leave their **burrow** to nibble grass.

CAN YOU REMEMBER?

Now you have read about some farm babies, can you remember their special names?

1.

2.

3.

4.

5.

6.

7.

8.

9.

10.

The answers are on page 31.

GLOSSARY

affection liking or loving another living thing

bank a raised strip of land by the side of a road or river

burrow an underground tunnel

calf a baby cow

caterpillar the young of a butterfly or moth

chick a baby bird

den an underground home made by an animal

down very soft feathers

duckling a baby duck

fawn a baby deer

fox cub a baby fox

gosling a baby goose

graze to eat grass that is growing in a meadow

groom cleaning an animal's fur

hatch to come out of an egg

headbutt to hit another animal (or person) hard with the head

hedgerow a line of trees and bushes along the side of a field or meadow

herd a group of animals living together

kid a baby goat

kitten a baby cat

lamb a baby sheep

mate when a male and female animal join together to have babies. Also the name for the partner of an animal.

nuzzle push gently against something

owlet a baby owl

piglet a baby pig

pregnancy the time when a female animal has its young developing inside its body

teat the part of a female animal's body that its young suck on to get milk

triplets three baby animals born to the same mother at the same time

twins two baby animals born to the same mother at the same time

udder the body part that makes milk

Answers
1. kid; 2. lamb; 3. owlets; 4. fox cub; 5. swallow chicks; 6. calf; 7. chick; 8. fawn; 9. duckling; 10. piglet

INDEX